From the first time I saw you, I knew you would have my heart. Happy Valentine's Day to the best wife I could have asked for

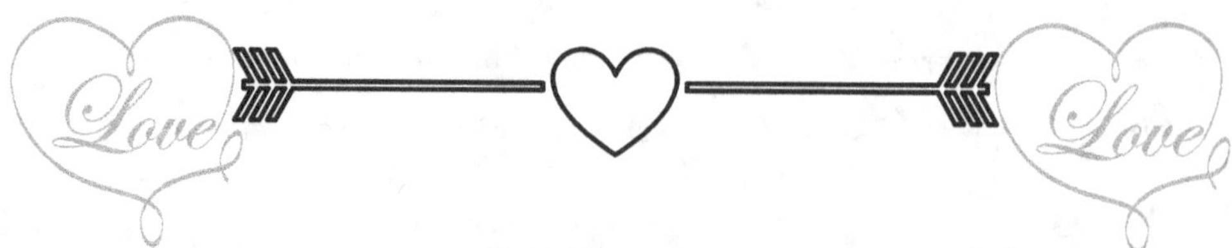